Amazing

Strong

Beautiful

I AM_____

REWRITE Your Name—REROUTE Your Life

Blessed

Fearless

Forgiven

CHRIS STEFANICK

real life
c a t h o l i c

Scripture passages are from the Revised Standard Version–Catholic Edition. Copyright © 1946, 1952, 1971, Division of Christian Education of the National Council of the Churches of Christ in the United States of America. All rights reserved.

Special thanks to James Stefanick for his vision and edits for this book, and for being a great father. And to Andrea Starosciak for her help in crafting reflection questions.

Cover design and layout by Mike Fontecchio, Faith & Family Publications. Cover title concept by Cassie Pease, Cassie Pease Designs.

Published by Jameson Press

For more information on this title and other books and CDs available through Real Life Catholic, please visit RealLifeCatholic.com.

ISBN: 978-0-9981688-1-4

Printed in the United States of America

Contents

"In the beginning was the Word."

-JOHN 1:1

THE *Power* OF THE *Word*

There's a war of words happening in your mind.
The outcome of that war determines your destiny.

There's a dialogue happening right now that's more important than any other in your life. It's the dialogue in your head. You spend a lot of time and energy wrestling with the voices in your head. Sometimes they speak in whispers too subtle to hear, but they're always there. And the way that dialogue pans out matters a lot.

The words you speak to yourself shape your self-perception. Your self-perception shapes your actions. Your actions shape your life. So the words you speak to yourself form the foundation of your whole life.

Where are the words you speak to yourself coming from? Self doubt? Old wounds? Echoes from past mistakes? Lack of affirmation that *should* have been there? A materialist culture? Or your Maker?

God has told us the truth about who we are. Liberating truth. Truth that breaks our bonds and sets us free. And that truth wasn't meant to remain on scrolls. God wants Scripture to rewrite the script in your head. He wants his Word to form the words you speak to yourself, how you see yourself, and how you live. But you have to do your part for that to happen.

DO YOUR PART

God didn't give us Sacred Scripture so we could wait for "professionals" to preach to us. He wants you to preach the truth to yourself. When that deflating voice in your head starts speaking up it's up to you to replace it with the voice of God. In the end, no one else can do that for you.

When you start thinking "I am weak. I am defeated. I am at the end of the line. I am unattractive. I am fat. I am unlovable." Think instead, "I am blessed. I am beautiful. I am chosen. I can do all things through Christ who strengthens me. I am more than a conqueror. And even in the hour of trial, GOD will never leave me or forsake me. I am beloved. I am fearfully and wonderfully made!" That's what God thinks about you. Those are the kinds of words that need to shape how you see yourself, how you act, and how you live.

It takes will, repetition, and practice to write a new script for the voice in your head. That's what this book is about.

The meditations in this book are designed to help you practice preaching to yourself. To give you daily infusions from God's word about your true identity—so that his Word can set a new and powerful direction for your life.

Each reflection begins with a new "I AM…" and a Scripture verse.

Here's a few simple ideas for how to use them as you work your way through this book:

- Post-its never get old. Invest in a few stacks and post the day's I AM someplace where you'll see it a few times.

- Pray with the I AM of the day. Read the day's Scripture quote, and then spend a few minutes in silence breathing in *I am* and breathing out your new name.

- Verbalize the day's "I AM" in a mirror." Literally. Look yourself in the eye and speak the truth. (Yes, I know, this one might feel a bit cheesy! But sometimes it helps to literally preach the truth to yourself out loud.)

- Tell a friend what you're doing and ask if you can call him or her every day to talk about what God is doing in your heart as you claim your new identity. It might end up helping your friend too. Better yet, get a group of friends together every week to read and discuss each "I AM." Use our questions as a guide!

- Broadcast your I AM and the day's Scripture quote for thirty-three days on social media. (Or please visit rewriteyourname.com and post our pre-made *I AM* memes. We got you covered!)

I could list ten more ideas but I'd rather keep it simple. God doesn't want to complicate your life and neither do I. There are also a few "homework" assignments at the end when you're done reading through all the meditations. Don't worry, they're simple ... but they're also important! So don't miss them!

I can't promise that a shift in your thinking will change all your circumstances or force certain blessings into your life.

I can think "I'm a millionaire" all day, but that doesn't put a penny in my pocket! What I *can* promise is that when you align your thinking with the Word of God something more important happens: it changes you. It makes you a happier, healthier, holier person. The rest is just details!

It's time to unlock the new "I AM" in your life. What are you waiting for? Turn the page.

"The truth will set you free."

—JOHN 8:32

"I am the truth."

—JOHN 14:6

I AM *New*

"*Therefore, if anyone is in Christ, he is a new
creation; the old has passed away.*"

—2 CORINTHIANS 5:17

*M*y Joey loves to ask me questions about when I was a boy. I think this is so that he can be sure that he will be like me when he's my age, and he wants to see if he's on the right track. (I'm lucky enough that my children overlook my flaws and look up to me! Kids are very merciful.)

"Dad, was your favorite color blue when you were my age?"

"Yes, Joey."

"Did you play ninjas?"

"Of course. I am one."

"Did you kill squirrels when you were a kid?"

"You killed a squirrel? Where? How!?"

"Ummm…Never mind!"

One time he stopped me and asked, "Dad, how do you remember when you were my age?"

Trying to explain the mystery of memory I said, "I don't know, Joey, how do you remember yesterday?" He said, "I don't remember yesterday."

Every day is new for a child, and every day should be new for a Christian. You have a right to "forget" about yesterday! You can always start over. Your past mistakes don't have to determine your future direction, nor do they sum up your identity. If you missed that point, you just missed the point of the Cross.

I recently had lunch with a former gang member who had converted to the Catholic Faith. He told me his story, how he used to get respect by hurting people: jumping people from rival gangs and beating them up with his fists, chains, and even stabbing them. He shared how he used to get a rush out of running from rivals who were trying to get even. All that changed when he found our Lord thanks to a Catholic gang outreach program called *Prevention y Rescate* (Prevention and Rescue).

As he spoke, his eyes were bright and pure. His face was gentle. I looked at him and said, "Angel (that's his name), I can't even see the guy you're describing. He's not in there any more. He's completely gone!"

Not only does our Lord forgive us, he remakes us. Reboots us. Repentance and confession make us like newborns. Such is the power of the Cross!

St. Paul—who used to hunt down Christians to have them killed but ended up penning more of the New Testament than anyone else—wrote that "anyone in Christ is a new Creation. The old has passed away."

> *"You shall be called by a new name which*
> *the mouth of the Lord will give."*
>
> —ISAIAH 62:2

YOU ARE A NEW CREATION. THE OLD IS GONE.
AND THE ONLY PERSON WITH THE POWER TO HOLD
THE PAST OVER YOUR HEAD IS YOU. STOP DOING THAT.

*What past mistakes are you holding onto
and letting define your identity?*

*Ask God to forgive you but most of all for the grace to let go
of the past and accept the new life he is waiting to give you.*

I AM *More*

*"And I tell you, you are Peter, and on this
rock I will build my Church."*

—MATTHEW 16:18

*S*imon didn't "have it all together", and that's how he perceived himself. In his first encounter with Jesus, he fell to his knees and said, "Get away from me, Lord. I'm a sinful man." Jesus gave him a new name, and like a signpost in his life that name was to point him in a radically new direction.

He took Simon and his apostles on a long journey from Galilee to Caesarea Philippi—an ancient pagan city on the border of modern-day Israel and Lebanon. I lead a yearly pilgrimage to the Holy Land, so I've made the journey before. But in the comfort of an air conditioned bus. It's a long trek on winding roads through very rugged, very hilly terrain. It must have been a grueling walk. But Jesus thought it was worth the long journey because it was the perfect backdrop for a very important conversation. There's a massive cliff of solid rock that looms over that ancient city, and Jesus didn't want Simon to forget that image as long as he lived.

There, before the massive slab of stone overshadowing the town, Jesus changed his chief apostle's name from Simon to Peter, which means "Rock."

He wanted that image seared into his mind: No little pebble, but the image of stability itself. He wanted Peter to think of that every time people said his name. "Good morning you massive Rock!" "Rock, would you please pass the fish?" Jesus knew that self-perception determines action, and he needed Peter to act as a rock solid leader for his Church.

Often, our negative self-images directly counter God's calling in our lives. God needed Peter to be a rock. The devil worked his whole life to make Peter see himself as broken and unstable.

Of course, Peter had flaws and weaknesses that persisted throughout his life, and he had to repent and work on them, just like us. But he was more than that. A negative guilt couldn't be the sum of his self-perception. After he met Jesus, "a sinful man" wasn't his name any more.

Stop listening to the Accuser. Combat him by claiming the opposite of his accusations. Have you dealt with feeling insecure? Jesus stands with you before a throne and says "Your name is King/Queen."

Do you feel dirty? He is at your side before a pool of the cleanest bluest water imaginable and he names you "Pure."

Feel powerless? "Behold the Mighty Tiger! That's you!" Anxious and out of control? "You are the Rock!"

Sure, you have flaws, but they don't sum up who you are. You are more than your flaws.

You've suffered setbacks, but those are pages in your life, not the whole story. You have wounds and weaknesses, but those don't define you.

You have sins, but they don't spell your name.

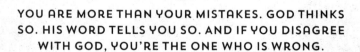

YOU ARE MORE THAN YOUR MISTAKES. GOD THINKS SO. HIS WORD TELLS YOU SO. AND IF YOU DISAGREE WITH GOD, YOU'RE THE ONE WHO IS WRONG.

What words and feelings does the devil use
to accuse you and shape your self-perception?

When these words and feelings come to mind, say out loud,
'Jesus says I am (opposite word/feeling), and his beloved.'
Slowly your mind will shift from the devil's lies
to the truth of who you are in Christ.

I AM *Lovable*

"For God so loved the world that he gave us his only Son…"

—JOHN 3:16

*y*ou are lovable. I know that because you are loved: infinitely and intimately.

If you want to know what God *really* thinks of you, the answer is: Jesus Christ. You have a God and Savior who thinks you're worth dying for. In fact, God made you so that he could love you! If that doesn't make you "lovable," I don't know what does!

The foundation of the Christian life lies in receiving love. He gives. We take and eat.

We often think that the spiritual life is all about the things we do for God. It's not. It's primarily about learning to receive what he did for us on the Cross, and continues to do for us by lavishing his grace on us every day. Everything we do as Christians is about cracking our hearts open wider and wider to receive the love that is God. Every service we render is a response to the love given us.

But to receive love you first have to claim that truth that you are lovable. Jesus told his followers to love others as they love themselves. He was presuming that the people following him love themselves!

Every time you dwell on a lie about who you are—a false identity that makes you feel ripped down, weak, or worthless, reply to that lie with the truth, "I am lovable. I know that because I am loved."

"But God shows his love for us in that while we were yet sinners Christ died for us."

—ROMANS 5:8

Name anything in your past or currently is preventing you from receiving God's love.

Make a list of the ways God has shown his love to you throughout your life.

I AM *Amazing*

"God created man in his own image."

—GENESIS 1:27

*M*y seven-year-old daughter recently asked me, "Daddy, why does the devil hate us?" I thought of the simplest answer I could give: "Because he hates God, and we look like God."

Her face lit up. "Wow! We look like God?!" As she said that I realized the profundity of what I'd just said! "Wow!" I said. "I guess we do!"

We're made in the image and likeness of God. Seeing that through the eyes of my child reminded me just how amazing that is.

God is creative and life-giving. So are you.

God is conscious and self-aware. You are too.

God is free. You have intellect and will.

God is love. You were made to give and receive love.

God is eternal. You will never end. You will outlast stars and galaxies. For all creation's majesty, those things can't be said about anything else. You. Look. Like. God.

When Adam first laid eyes on Eve—her deep, intelligent eyes, walking upright with grace, gentle and responsive to the world all around her yet bearing a dignity that says, "I am master over all this"—he may have been tempted for a moment to bow down and worship. As the Psalmist says, "You have made us little less than a god" (Psalm 8:5).

I'm not sure what to add to all that except to say, "Wow."

You've probably been amazed at mountains, oceans, and stars. What about yourself? Stop for a minute today and marvel at the wonder of you (and while you're at it, the wonder of other people in your life). I'm sure God will.

"Then God said, 'Let us make man in our image, after our likeness; and let them have dominion over the fish of the sea, and over the birds of the air, and over the cattle, and over all the earth.'"

—GENESIS 1:26

Spend a minute reflecting on the attributes you like the most about yourself. How do these gifts from God reflect his image?

Look at your schedule for the upcoming week and identify two people you will meet. Spend a few minutes reflecting on what's special about them, and how God builds you up through them. Tell them how you appreciate their presence in your life.

I AM *Chosen*

"'Follow me, and I will make you fishers of men.'
Immediately they left their nets and followed him."

—MATTHEW 4:19-20

When I was a kid, there was a painful ritual every week on the playground. When it was time to play kickball, two team captains took turns picking their players. The least athletic kids were always picked last. I was generally at the bottom of the barrel with them! Humiliating.

A worse process happened at every high school dance, as countless lonely hearts waited with baited breath to be asked by someone, and after a while, anyone. Please pick me!

We all want to be chosen. To be special. Some things never change.

In Jesus' time, rabbis regularly made their rounds through towns teaching Jewish children the faith until they were fourteen. When they turned fourteen they were either told to learn their father's trade, or they were set apart with the words, "Come, follow me." The specially chosen ones would leave everything and follow their rabbi.

They would spend years learning from him. And they didn't just learn theological lessons. They would be with him all the time, watching his every move. They came to love the things he loved and reject the things he rejected. They learned to see the world through his eyes. They didn't only learn to pray and teach with his words, they learned to pray and teach with his heart. And by the time they were rabbis themselves, they were mirror images of their master.

I think the apostles had each wanted to be chosen to follow a rabbi when they were fourteen, but that ship had sailed. "Pick me!" they thought. But they were told to go home and work their father's trade.

Imagine their shock when the greatest rabbi ever broke into their world with the words "Come, follow me."

You haven't been looked over, you know. He has picked you and called you on an interior journey. A lifelong daily journey that will bring you so close to him that you become his mirror image. Out of all the people on the earth he has spoken your name. "Sonya. Ethan. Ryan. Natalie. James. [Insert your name here.] Come, follow me."

You are chosen.

"THERE WAS ONCE A LITTLE PRINCESS WHO..."

"BUT, MR. AUTHOR, WHY DO YOU ALWAYS
WRITE ABOUT PRINCESSES?"

"BECAUSE EVERY LITTLE GIRL IS A PRINCESS."

"YOU WILL MAKE THEM VAIN IF YOU TELL THEM THAT."

"NOT IF THEY UNDERSTAND WHAT I MEAN."

"THEN WHAT DO YOU MEAN BY A PRINCESS?"

"THE DAUGHTER OF A KING."

—GEORGE MACDONALD, *THE PRINCESS AND THE GOBLIN*

Do you think your being chosen depends on your performance, success, looks…or the unconditional love of God?

Reflect on how free you would be if you felt truly chosen by God, not based on what you accomplish but just because of who you are. Ask God to help you live in that space today!

DAY 6

I AM *Bold*

"Then Moses stretched out his hand over the sea...
and the waters were divided."

—EXODUS 14:21

W e pray too small.

"Lord, help me to just hang in there today. Help me not crumble under the pressures of life."

Is that all you think God is capable of?

We don't have a God of "just getting by." We don't have a God of "just barely enough." We have a God of life to the full!

We have a God who didn't just create a place for us to dwell. We have a God who went overboard and set a trillion galaxies in motion as the backdrop for where we would meet him.

We don't have a God who gave us a little glimpse of his love. We have a God of the Cross and Resurrection. We don't have a God who sometimes helps his people out. We have a God who splits seas, conquered death, moves hearts, and makes heroes. That's the power and love you're tapping into when you pray. *Extravagant* is God's middle name.

What is it about the way he created or redeemed us that tells you to ask small?!

Instead of asking for a drip of water, why not ask for rivers of living water to flow from within you to a thirsty world? Instead of asking God to help your marriage, why not ask him to empower you to sweep your wife off her feet again? Instead of asking him to help you not crumble under peer pressure (which impacts adults as much as kids!), why not ask him to make you a blazing light shining before everyone you know?

Why not that?

I know...it's because you think God is small. You think you're small. Stop it. Our God is not small. Neither are his children. He is almighty, and you are his.

Be bold.

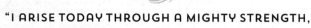

"I ARISE TODAY THROUGH A MIGHTY STRENGTH, THE INVOCATION OF THE TRINITY, THROUGH BELIEF IN THE THREENESS, THROUGH CONFESSION OF THE ONENESS OF THE CREATOR OF CREATION."

—ST. PATRICK

What prayers do you want to pray but haven't,
thinking that God can't or won't answer big prayers?

Ask the Lord today for a fresh set of faithful eyes to see his majesty,
ability, and desire to answer bold prayers, and ask big today!

I AM *Forgiven*

"While he was yet at a distance, his father saw him and had compassion, and ran and embraced him and kissed him."

—LUKE 15:20

*A*s I shared in the best selling book *Joy to the World*, I got locked in a knock-down-drag-out "conversation" with one of my teens. Not a physical fight, God forbid, but an upsetting verbal one. (If you have teens of your own, you're not judging me right now.)

As can happen to the best of us, he had momentarily lost control over his mouth. I found myself thinking, "I can't believe my kid is talking to me this way." As the conversation went from bad to worse, I realized that he was thinking the same thing. "I can't believe I'm saying this to my dad!" I could see that his own words were starting to hurt him.

I had a grace-filled moment where I switched from parental rage to compassion. I interrupted him and said, "I forgive you." He kept talking, so I said it louder. "I forgive you." He kept talking, so I hugged him and said a third time, "I forgive you." His rant turned to tears. "I'm sorry, dad."

That's the Cross. It's God crying out to a broken humanity, "I forgive you. Just accept it." We over complicate what we need to do to be forgiven. God doesn't.

We hold on to our sins. God doesn't.

We consider the intricate web of all the people our sins have hurt and we think we need to pay the price. God doesn't.

He paid the price for us.

He's buried our sins at the bottom of the ocean (see Micah 7:10).

As far as the east is from the west, that's how far he's removed our guilt from us (see Psalm 103:12).

Jesus loves to hear your songs of praise. Know what he loves to hear more than that? Your worst sin. He died on a cross so he could hear your worst, most shameful secret and so you could hear in return, "I absolve you in the name of the Father, and of the Son, and of the Holy Spirit." He died on a cross so you could let your head collapse on your father's chest, choke out a few tears, and say "I'm sorry, dad" with the full knowledge that forgiveness is already waiting for you.

Mercy and forgiveness is Love's response to your brokenness. The cross is proof. Claim that truth.

You may have heard the words of forgiveness from God. Be sure to speak them to yourself, in cooperation with him. Look in the mirror and say it out loud if you have to: "I forgive myself of my worst sin. Even if I don't feel forgiven, I forgive myself because God has forgiven me. I believe in the forgiveness of sins. I believe that I am forgiven!"

YESTERDAY IS GONE. TOMORROW HAS NOT YET COME. WE HAVE ONLY TODAY. LET US BEGIN.

—ST. TERESA OF CALCUTTA (MOTHER TERESA)

What sin do you have a difficult time believing God has forgiven?
Think about this: Do you really think that mistake
is bigger than God's power to forgive?

End each day by asking God to forgive you, and more, ask him to
help you forgive yourself. And try to get to confession regularly,
at least once a month. The grace is amazing, but so is the
psychological experience of venting your sins in that safe space.

I AM *Royalty*

"[We are] heirs of God and fellow heirs with Christ, provided we
suffer with him in order that we may also be glorified with him."

—ROMANS 8:17

There's a special red disk in the entryway floor of St. Peter's Basilica in Rome. Almost 1,700 years ago, it was in front of the altar, and it's the stone where emperors and kings like the great Charlemagne knelt for their coronations.

When St. Peter's was renovated and rebuilt about four hundred years ago, that very disk was carefully preserved and moved to the entryway. Something that kings knelt on is now there for every Christian to walk over as they enter the house of God. That wasn't done to insult the kings of the past but to honor the Christians of the present. It was decided that every pilgrim who enters St. Peter's should be reminded of his or her great dignity.

In baptism, we are anointed "priest, prophet, and king" in Christ. That's because Jesus doesn't just redeem us. He raises us up and shares his high office with us!

I recently learned of a woman whose daughter had Down Syndrome and died at a young age. She told her daughter, "You're a princess," and the little girl would tell everyone she met, "I am the daughter of a great king!" One day she looked intently at her mom and said, "Mommy, you have a crown, but you don't see it."

Friend, you are a son or daughter of the King of the Universe. You are about to inherit an imperishable kingdom. You have a crown. You desperately need to start seeing it, and acting like it.

"EVERY LITTLE GIRL IS A PRINCESS, AND THERE WOULD BE NO NEED TO SAY ANYTHING ABOUT IT, EXCEPT THAT SHE IS ALWAYS IN DANGER OF FORGETTING HER RANK AND BEHAVING AS IF SHE HAD GROWN OUT OF THE MUD. I HAVE SEEN LITTLE PRINCESSES BEHAVE LIKE THE CHILDREN OF THIEVES AND LYING BEGGARS, AND THAT IS WHY THEY NEED TO BE TOLD THEY ARE PRINCESSES."

—GEORGE MACDONALD, *THE PRINCESS AND THE GOBLIN*

How does your life fail to reflect the reality of your dignity?

What are you going to do about it? Start here: Upon waking every morning, look at yourself in the mirror and say "I am a royal [son or daughter] of the Most High God."

I AM *Fearless*

"Fear not, little flock, for it is your Father's good pleasure to give you the kingdom."

—LUKE 12:32

*F*ear is a murderer. It stops us from living. Much of Jesus' ministry was about conquering our fears. He turned the lights on and opened the closet, showing us that, in the end, there's no boogie man hiding in our room that's bigger than he is, not even death.

St. John Paul II had good reason to live in fear. He lost his mom when he was eight, big brother when he was twelve, and came home to find his father dead on the floor when he was twenty. As an old man reflecting on his youth he said, "Before my twenty-first birthday, I had already lost all the people I loved."

In addition to human frailty, he experienced the full weight of human evil. He lived in the epicenter of all the suffering of the twentieth century. He watched his homeland be turned into a Nazi slave state when he was a teen. His house was a short, thirty-minute drive from Auschwitz. By the end of World War II, one-fifth of his countrymen had died, including some of his best friends. Then Poland was taken over by communists who hated his people and his faith as much as the Nazis did. He would serve as a bishop under their watchful eyes and constant threats.

Yet his personal motto (though not his official papal motto) was the command Jesus spoke more than any other in Scripture:

"Be not afraid!" Jesus said those words 365 times in the Gospels, once for each day of the year! He knew we have much to fear, but from his eternal perspective, we have absolutely no reason to be fearful.

John Paul II chose to meditate on and claim that truth instead of letting tragedy upon tragedy chase him away from the experience of life. And he had a joy, optimism, peace, and boldness about him that, frankly, confounded the world!

What are you afraid of? How is it stopping you from living?

Some people are so afraid of themselves they never face their own wounds; so afraid of death they never live; so afraid of being hurt they never expose their hearts to others; so afraid of failure they never take risks; so afraid of conflicts they let relationships die instead.

God is inviting you to live life to the full, but you need to trust him to live that life. He is bigger than your bogeyman. Be not afraid.

"For the weapons of our warfare are not worldly but have divine power to destroy strongholds. We destroy arguments and every proud obstacle to the knowledge of God, and take every thought captive to obey Christ."

—2 CORINTHIANS 10:4-5

Reflect on the past year of your life. How has fear robbed you and how would your life be different if you weren't afraid?

Make a list of your current fears and set aside a couple of minutes each day to speak aloud "Because of Jesus' love for me, I am entrusting my fear of [fear name] to him." By releasing your fears to him on a daily basis, he will transform them into badges of Faith.

I AM *Favored*

"Hail, full of grace, the Lord is with you!"

—LUKE 1:28

I met a woman who had suffered over ten miscarriages. Tragedy upon tragedy taught her a lie: "I am cursed." She carried that lie around in the secret of her heart but with a smile ever on her face. Inside, she was imprisoned by it.

Lies about who we are often attach themselves to our pain. Tragedies can convince us we have been forgotten at best, cursed at worse.

Christian theology and the lives of countless saints and heroes shows us the truth about suffering. Suffering is what chisels heroic souls out from the rest of us. I wish there was another way. I would love to be the patron saint of people who sit on a beach and sip a Corona, but saints are born of sagas. In his human nature, Jesus himself was "made perfect by what he suffered" (Hebrews 2:10).

The central image of Christian faith, hanging prominently in every parish, is a man in agony. We don't have a God who promised us freedom from pain. He promised his presence in our pain. He didn't suffer so we wouldn't have to. He suffered so we would know how to. Pain will make us bitter or better. Which of the two is up to us.

The woman with the miscarriages knew all that. She had been active in ministry for years. But those were no more than lofty ideas that didn't apply to her, because she had forgotten the truth about who she was.

"I am cursed."

That lie had seeped like a poison into every other area of her life and she didn't even know it. Our lies are often subtle. They lie below the surface just enough for us not to really notice them, while they rob us of our joy.

She claimed her new identity at a talk I gave at her parish. There were no complex theological insights in my talk. It was a very simple theme: God loves you, gave himself up for you, and calls you to give your life to him in return. It was the basic Gospel message. She had heard it before, but it struck her in a new way that night.

She came up to me afterwards in tears. "I thought I was cursed. I've been operating under a lie I didn't even know was there. I carried that lie around for so many years. I realized tonight that I'm not cursed! I'm his beloved daughter!"

Are you facing a tragedy? Is your heart or body aching right now? If so, I'm so sorry. Please don't add to that pain the lie that you're cursed! You're not forgotten. You're not abandoned. You're not cursed. You're especially chosen for greatness. In hard times, you are his highly favored. Believe it! It's true.

"We rejoice in our sufferings, knowing that suffering produces endurance, and endurance produces character, and character produces hope."

—ROMANS 5:3-4

*Name a tragedy in your life that makes you
feel cursed, forgotten, or abandoned.*

*How does your view of this tragedy change with the
knowledge that Jesus suffers with us and teaches us how to
offer our suffering back to God as an act of love?*

I AM *Powerful*

"*Behold, I have given you authority to tread upon serpents and scorpions, and over all the power of the enemy; and nothing shall hurt you.*"

—LUKE 10:19

xorcisms are still performed to this day, though only after extensive psychological examinations and evidence of supernatural activity—which is less rare than one might think. A friend of mine was on a mission trip to Haiti with a German and a Russian when an uneducated, possessed woman who only spoke Creole cursed them fluently in their three different languages. Sadly, this stuff is still very real.

What strikes me about the people I've met who are involved in exorcism ministry is how calm and cool they are. Demons often spout out lies mixed with truths at exorcists—often about their personal lives. I know of exorcists laughing in response. They're about as scared and awe inspired by dark spirits as an exterminator is by the rats he's kicking out of a house. No doubt, they're big, freaky, invisible rats, but that's all they are. The exorcist is able to put evil in its place because he's aware that God is bigger than any spiritual rat. A Christian with the indwelling presence of God, calling on his name, has authority—enough authority to terrify demons.

Before an exorcism is complete, the priest has to dig out the "rat's" name, and command it, by name, to go back to where it came from, never to return.

Not to freak you out: but there's often a spiritual dimension to the lies that have attached themselves to you. The good news is that you have the authority, as a son or daughter of God with his indwelling presence, to renounce that lie and *the liar* and send it back to where it came from!

As St. Paul writes, "[We] take every thought captive to obey Christ" (2 Corinthians 10:5). We have that power!

Whenever I meet someone at an event who comes up to me and shares that they have been imprisoned by a lie, I pray with them and we renounce the lie together, out loud. Spiritual or not, that lie is an enemy, but when you stand with Christ, you're strong enough to defeat it.

"We are not contending against flesh and blood, but against the principalities, against the powers, against the rulers of this present darkness, against the spiritual hosts of wickedness in heavenly places."

—EPHESIANS 6:12

*Do you see a spiritual theme in the lies
that have attached themselves to you?*

*Ask Jesus in prayer to help you believe the authority you have
as a child of God over these lies. Then out loud, renounce each
lie by name and ask Jesus to take them captive. Read Psalm 91
to remind yourself of God's protection over your life.*

DAY 12

I AM *Valuable*

*"You know that you were ransomed from the futile ways
inherited from your fathers, not with perishable things such
as silver or gold, but with the precious blood of Christ."*

—1 PETER 1:18-19

*T*he devil's been lying about something for a long time. The lie has taken many forms over the course of history. To sum up the lie: "You have worth, dignity, purpose, and value *if*. . ."

The Nazis said, "You have rights *if* you're a member of the Aryan race." The communists say, "You have dignity *if* you contribute to society." The secular humanists say, "You have purpose *if* you make it up for yourself." The architects behind social media say, "You matter *if* people notice." The materialists say, "You have value *if* you own enough stuff and wear the right thing."

But it's all the same lie from the same dark source, and it all ends in death: from the bodily death of the gas chamber or the gulag, the business man who takes a dive from a ten-story window when his stock crashes, or the teen suicide, to the spiritual death of those who wander through life not knowing who they are, or why they are, or if they matter at all.

God's word tells us we have dignity, purpose, and value, not *if* but *because.*

One of my children asked me why I loved them and why I was proud of him. He qualified his question with "and don't just say it's because I'm your dad and you're my kid! I want *real* reasons!"

I gave him reasons and praised his good qualities, but then clarified, "And do you think those reasons make you worthy of my love? What better reason could there possibly be for me to love you and be proud of you than the fact that you're my son? Do you think something you can *do* or *accomplish* would be a better reason? You are mine. That's why I love you.

That is why God loves us too. "You are mine" (Isaiah 43:1).

Your value in terms of accomplishments or sums of money will never measure up to the value you already have in his eyes. You are so infinitely valuable that God, in his infinite majesty, he found you worth dying for. The Cross reveals your true "net worth!"

"You are all children of the light and of the day. You belong neither to night nor to darkness."

—1 THESSALONIANS 5:5

*Do you measure your self-worth according to the
world's standards (beauty, money, notoriety, power)?
How would your life be better if you didn't?*

Today, say, "God loves me for me, *not for what I can do, what I have,
or how I look but because I am his." Google the "Suscipe" prayer
by St. Ignatius of Loyola to claim detachment from the world
and attachment to God's imperishable love for you.*

I AM *Strong*

"For I will all the more gladly boast of my weaknesses,
that the power of Christ may rest upon me...
for when I am weak, then I am strong."

—2 CORINTHIANS 12:9-10

Ski jumping amazes me. It's crazy. The world record, held by Anders Fannimel of Norway is 251.5 meters. That's 825 feet soaring through the air, face first...with skis on.

Countless hours of training are behind a jump like that. The skier has to learn all the mechanics and "how to's." But for every jumper, there's got to be that moment when he faces his first *real* jump. Not just the kiddie jump, but the kind where there's so much speed upon take off that you have to angle your body parallel to the ground once you catch air. No amount of training can make you push off down that slope. In the end, only confidence can do that. And then you soar, or you learn a painful lesson and try again!

I've been in over my head countless times. I've spoken to arenas filled with more than 25,000 people. I've been on radio and TV, and even filmed a TV series. And I've often had this nagging sense that I wasn't remotely qualified for what I was about to do. Sure, I've spoken to people, but I didn't have experience at any of those things before I did them the first time.

And every time I've had to face down the nagging doubts: "Are you crazy?", "Who do you think you are?", "You're not qualified to do that!", "If you make an idiot out of yourself in front of 25,000 people do you know how many people are going to see it? 25,000!"

We all face those moments in life that push us out of our safe space and into the wide open: from leaving home for college, to a risky career move, to standing up for what's right, to speaking in front of a live audience, to an actual ski jump!

And every time we'll hear the voice, "Are you crazy! Sit down, take those skis off, and stay where it's safe."

Maybe that voice is from the Evil One, who is terrified of us becoming who we're meant to be. Maybe it's the old voice of detractors echoing in your mind. Maybe it's the voice that rises from the gap where a parent or coach didn't empower you. Or maybe it's the very rational voice of self-preservation! No matter. When that voice starts to paralyze me with fear and anxiety, I know it's time to dig deep. When I come face to face with my own weakness, I know it's time to draw strength from a love that's bigger than I am.

I sit in silent prayer and recall the people who have shown me the love of God, the people I feel fully myself around, the people who make me feel safe just being me, like my mom and dad. I remember the people who don't ever gauge my worth on my successes or failings, and who will love me regardless of whether the world ever reads the words I'm writing right now. I soak in how they've made me feel. I rejoice in the feeling of "solid" and of warm light they put deep in my gut. I thank God for them. I thank God for the way he has showed me HIS love through them.

Then I remember the people who have loved me very conditionally. The people who have ripped me down or made me feel small. I reject the feeling of "hollow"—the cool, dark pit they deposited deep in my gut. And with the most magnanimous spirit I can muster, I forgive them. I release them.

Then, I'm ready to jump! Not because I'm strong on my own. Not because I'm 100% sure I'll succeed. But because a child who knows he's *really* loved isn't afraid of failure anyway.

Name the experiences and people that make you feel small,
inadequate, and unworthy. Ask God to help you re-frame these
experiences to one of forgiveness of those who hurt you.

Spend time visualizing how God loves and strengthens you through others.
Thank him for each of the people who came to mind by name.
Pray this prayer frequently and be amazed at the strength you gain!

I AM *Marvelous*

"My soul magnifies the Lord."

—LUKE 1:46

*A*t the risk of sounding silly: I am marvelous! That is, *worthy of being marveled at,* or as Google dictionary says, *"causing great wonder."*

Mary, the model disciple, clearly thought that about herself. Much of her famous prayer from the first chapter of Luke, the Magnificat isn't just about God. It's about her.

"My soul magnifies the Lord." That was the start of Mary's prayer when she had Jesus in her womb and met Elizabeth who was pregnant with Jesus' cousin, John the Baptist.

In a stunned and grace-filled moment, realizing "the presence" in Mary, Elizabeth blurted out, "Who am I that the mother of my Lord should come to me?", and then the prayer that would be uttered by Catholics the world over, "Blessed art thou among women and blessed is the fruit of thy womb!"

This encounter may have been the first time Mary's head stopped spinning since the conception of the Second Person of the Trinity (God the Son), by the power of the Third Person (God the Holy Spirit), and eternal plan of the First Person (God the Father). And she marveled. She was blown away.

She burst into one of the most beautiful songs of praise in salvation history. The beauty of the Magnificat lies in the fact that there was something very different about this song of praise. Mary didn't just rejoice in the greatness of God *in himself* but the greatness of God in her.

And so she prayed, "All generations will call me blessed!"

God wants you to marvel at yourself that way too—at the way that he shines uniquely and unrepeatably through you, and you alone. He wants you to consider the particular virtues, and all that's beautiful, good, and true in YOU. He wants you to smile about the gifts that only you can bring into the lives of other people. And he wants you to respond with the joy and freedom of a child: "MY soul proclaims the greatness of the Lord!"

Mary was blown away—by God, by herself, by God all wrapped up in herself. And she prayed like King David, "I praise you, because I am wonderfully made; wonderful are your works!" (Psalm 139:14).

Have you ever thought of yourself this way?

"At that very moment he rejoiced [in] the holy Spirit and said, 'I give you praise, Father, Lord of heaven and earth, for although you have hidden these things from the wise and the learned you have revealed them to the childlike. Yes, Father, such has been your gracious will.'"

—LUKE 10:21

Take a moment to marvel at your fingerprints. There is no one else in the history of mankind who has or will ever have your fingerprints. If God made this "insignificant" part of you unique and unrepeatable, ponder the greatness He has poured into the rest of your life.

Reach out to a friend today and tell that person a particular gift or aspect of her/his personality that you think is a blessing.

I AM *Capable*

"I can do all things in [Christ] who strengthens me."

—PHILIPPIANS 4:13

When the apostles saw Jesus walking on water they were terrified. They thought it was a ghost. Peter blurted out, "If it's you, Lord, tell me to come to you."

He was looking for a miracle as proof. But since an evil spirit might have been able to pull that off, I think Peter was also looking for something more.

There was something about Jesus' voice when he talked to Peter that was unmistakable for him, and maybe unlike any other voice in Peter's life: you see, Peter didn't just believe in Jesus. Jesus believed in Peter.

"Tell me to walk on water. Tell me I can do it and I'll know it's you." "Come."

When Peter heard Jesus tell him to walk on the water, he was sure it wasn't a ghost. It was the voice that built him up. It was the Lord.

There are voices in your life, too.

Empowering experiences throughout life are a "voice" that builds us up. Everything from my dad giving me a shovel and sending me out into the snow to singlehandedly rescue our driveway from a blizzard, to him teaching me to properly swing a stick and then throwing a ball at me—it all communicates:

"You're a man. You're capable. Go for it. You can do it! And if you fail, it's okay."

Negative experiences are a different voice. Everything from a bully who ripped me down, to a teacher who just didn't like me—it all communicates: "You're small. Incapable. If you want to venture out and do what's burning in your heart, you need to wait for everyone else's permission, or God forbid you crumble and fail in front of everyone and look like a fool!"

Do yourself a favor and stop listening to the choir of critical voices that keeps ripping you down. Those voices aren't from God. Those aren't his angels.

GOD is giving you permission. Go. Do. Conquer. You can!

"Come."

"Be transformed by the renewal of your mind."

—ROMANS 12:2

What negative words have held you back the most?
Who spoke them? Visualize them written on a scroll script.

Now imagine Jesus asking you to come to him.
Visualize him taking that script, ripping it up, and handing
you a new one. What is written on the script he gave you?

I AM *Claimed*

*"The Lord has chosen you to be a people for his own possession,
out of all the peoples that are on the face of the earth."*

—DEUTERONOMY 14:2

I know a woman whose parents divorced when she was seven. Despite their best intentions, the experience of bouncing from house to house for parental visits planted a lie in her soul: "I have to fend for myself."

When she was a preteen she suffered from sexual abuse while her parents were at work. The lie embedded itself deeper. "There is no one to care for you."

As a teen, it was easy for her to get away with things and hard for her parents to keep her in line. But the wild life she indulged in was a cry, "See, mom and dad, no limits! You can't stop me, and that means you can't protect me." And they couldn't protect her—not from herself.

What she learned at the age of seven followed her well into adulthood: "There's no one to care for you." The fruit of that lie is a spirit of control to the point of exhaustion. She had to be in the driver's seat. If she wasn't in control, after all, who was? And while that made her look strong on the outside, it was all a shell protecting a weak, wounded, and overwhelmed soul. She was just a seven-year-old in a thirty-something body looking to be held, protected, and told that everything is going to be alright. It took years of counseling to uproot and heal the wounds of her childhood.

Like countless others, she grew up with one of the Evil One's favorite lies echoing in her ears: "There is no one to care for you. You're an orphan that no one picked. You're fatherless."

That lie in my friend's story is easily seen, but the same lie can embed itself in us in the subtlest ways, and it's no less harmful. In our family of six children we've had to guard against that lie creeping into our toddler's hearts every time a new infant comes along! "Have I been replaced? Am I on my own now?"

Deep within there is a need to have a father who sets you apart, sits you on his knee, looks you in the eye, embraces you, and tells you everything is going to be alright because he loves you. And he's strong. We all need that. But none of our earthly fathers and mothers can adequately give that to us, because in the end, what we seek is perfect love from a limitless power. One that can shield us with his embrace even when we walk through the valley of the shadow of death. "See? Even here I am with you. Everything is going to be alright."

YOU'RE NOT FATHERLESS. EVEN IF YOU'RE AN ORPHAN, YOUR GOD IS AN ALL POWERFUL, ALL LOVING FATHER. YOU'RE PROVIDED FOR, CARED FOR, AND SAFE. YOU'RE CLAIMED.

---

*How has the love you have received from your earthly family
shaped your perception of God's fatherly love and care for you?*

*Following the example of St. Thérèse of Lisieux, schedule time
this week in silent prayer, visualizing God holding you as a child.
Drop the defenses you have constructed and allow yourself to
become very small. Say out loud "My Father, the Maker of
the Universe has claimed me. I am his and he is mine."*

I AM
Broken and Shared

*"Jesus took bread, and blessed, and broke it, and gave it
to the disciples and said, 'Take, eat; this is my body.'"*

—MATTHEW 26:26

*g*rowing up on the rugged Australian frontier in the 1800s wasn't easy for St. Mary Mackillop. Her father had a fatal flaw: he failed at every business venture he attempted. By the age of fourteen, she was helping provide for her eight younger siblings.

She discovered that she had a gift for teaching children. That gift went from a career to a sacred calling. She took vows and became a religious sister and educator who committed her whole life to helping other families who were struggling on the frontier as she had. Within about five years, her passion ignited a movement. More than 120 women joined her as religious sisters and teachers.

But her new community was misunderstood so badly by Church leadership that Mary was excommunicated. Ouch. Her response was gracious and obedient, but she never gave up. She managed to get the official blessing and approval of the pope himself.

By the time she died, Mary had 750 sisters serving 12,500 students in 117 schools.

Think about the qualities Mary needed to be a blessing to the world: her grit, her patience, her perseverance, her compassion for people in hard circumstances. If she had it easy growing up, she probably wouldn't have had any of those qualities. God wasn't able to use her *despite* the things she suffered in life, but precisely *because* of those things. God transformed her brokenness into a blessings for others. That's the story of countless saints.

Sometimes God closes the wounds of our past. Other times, he transforms them into resurrected wounds—like the kind he had when he emerged from the tomb after passing through death. You could still see the signs of the cross on his body, but the holes in his hands were now a source of healing for a broken world.

"All things work together for good to those who love God" (Romans 8:28). ALL things. Your wounds aren't to remain your weaknesses. God has plans to turn your brokenness into blessing. Think of your wounds that way.

SIN. DISEASE. ABUSE. TRAGEDY. THOSE DO NOT SUM UP THE STORY OF YOUR LIFE. THOSE ARE JUST PAGES. THERE IS A BIGGER STORY.

Invite the Lord into the painful memories of your life by praying,
"Jesus, if only [name the suffering] hadn't happened."

Think of how the sufferings you identified above have strengthened you,
enabled you to be a more compassionate person, or have helped you
help others. Then re-frame the pain in prayer by saying,
"Jesus, if [name the suffering] hadn't happened, I wouldn't
[name the blessing]." Do this with each new wound God allows
into your life and slowly you will only see them as blessings.

I AM *Me*

*"God saw everything that he had made,
and behold, it was very good."*

—GENESIS 1:31

When I was three, my mother asked me who I wanted to be when I grew up. I looked at her confused, paused, and then said with furrowed brow, "A big-one Christopher."

In other words: "I want to be myself. Obviously."

I wish I could say I always remembered that. Too many times in life I've wanted to be someone else. Comparison is one of the devil's favorite tricks. And envy is one of the dumbest sins in his arsenal. It's the only sin that has absolutely no pleasure attached to it. Yet we're dumb enough to fall into it!

I've envied. I've compared myself with others countless times. I've set the successes of others as my personal career goals. I've mistakenly wanted to bless the world with other people's gifts! While all along, God was just calling me to be me.

That kind of striving is joy draining as well as stifling. I couldn't write until I gave up my preconceived notions of what a religious book *should* be like. I'm not C.S. Lewis or J.R.R. Tolkien. I'm not Scott Hahn or Jeff Cavins. I'm not St. John Paul II. And when I try to be, I stink at it. God's calling me to find my own path—my own voice.

I'm not saying we shouldn't look up to others. There are lots of saints, theologians, family, and friends who I consider personal heroes. But God has set them before me as inspirations, not molds. I'm called to be fully and completely me.

One of the many amazing things about being made in the image and likeness of God is that, among many other qualities, it means you are a *conscious center*. You see the universe through your eyes. Experience the world with your heart. Think with your mind. You and you alone can say of yourself, "I am me." Not even God with all his power, has the power to be you. So then, be YOU!

To be holy is to be whole. It's to be fully alive. Completely YOU.

In the words of Oscar Wilde, "Be yourself; everyone else is already taken." In the words of St. Catherine of Siena, "Be who God meant you to be and you will set the world on fire." And in the words of three-year-old me, "I want to be a big-one Christopher."

"IT IS NOT THE MOUNTAIN WE CONQUER, BUT OURSELVES."

—SIR EDMUND HILLARY

Analyze the goals you have for your life. In what ways have you been striving to be someone else, or to live someone else's life instead of your own?

Spend time in gratitude for YOU today: Who God made you and what he has given you. Thank him for everything that comes to mind. You'll be amazed the contentment that comes from that kind of gratitude!

I AM *Consecrated*

"The Lord has set apart his faithful servant for himself."

—PSALM 4:3

To consecrate something is to set it aside for a special purpose, usually through a ritual. When a priest wants to make holy water, he blesses it. That water is then set aside for holy things. It's no longer for a water bottle. It's for baptisms and blessing.

Churches are consecrated buildings. There's a beautiful ritual to set them apart wherein the altar is covered in holy oils by a bishop. And there's a ritual to deconsecrate them if they're closed permanently or sold.

A married couple is consecrated in a ceremony. They're set apart for one another. As the author of Song of Songs says, "I am my beloved's and my beloved is mine" (Songs 6:3). That's not just poetry. Marriage is a bond sealed by a vow unto death. Man and woman become holy vessels of God's grace for one another and the world as God enters their love in a new way.

At Mass, the word "consecration" refers to what happens when the priest prays the words, "This is my body" over the bread, turning it into the body of Christ. It's no longer bread.

Did you know that *you* are consecrated? When you were baptized you were set apart. Chosen. Water was poured over you and you were claimed for Christ. When you were sealed with the power of the Holy Spirit at confirmation, you were anointed with oil like a church altar. When you received the Eucharist, you were further consecrated as God joined himself to you in the flesh. You are set apart, made holy. Your life has a sacred purpose. You are a temple where God lives and where people encounter his presence. In fact, the only reason anything else is consecrated in the Church is so that you can be.

"You were washed, you were sanctified, you were justified in the name of the Lord Jesus Christ and by the Spirit of our God."

—1 CORINTHIANS 6:11

Spend time in silent prayer, visualizing the moments of your baptism and confirmation. Look at yourself in the mirror and say, "I am consecrated and set apart in the name of the Father, and of the Son, and of the Holy Spirit!"

The next time you receive the Eucharist at Mass, reflect for a moment not just on the holiness of God, or the church you're in, but of yourself, made holy by the indwelling presence of God.

I AM

Kind of a Big Deal

"What is man that you are mindful of him, and the son of man that you care for him? Yet you have made him little less than God, and have crowned him with glory and honor. You have given him dominion over the works of your hands; you have put all things under his feet."

—PSALM 8:4-6

There are hundreds of billions of stars in our galaxy and according to the latest estimates there are two trillion galaxies in the universe. When you think about that, it's easy to feel insignificant and small.

Obviously, the universe is a very vast place! Some people consider the enormity of it all and conclude that there's no God and that we're just a cosmic accident. As if the enormity of the universe disproves the existence of a mighty God! Other people think that if there is a God, he couldn't possibly think of us—small as we are. As if vast amounts of matter, energy, and empty space have greater cosmic significance than you!

You might look up at the stars and planets and sky and feel small, but I can assure you that your Maker is looking down and thinking that you are huge next to all that!

Even on a physical level, you are magnificent. Sure, there are billions upon billions of stars in the universe, but there are 100 trillion living cells in your body. Each, in its own way, more magnificent than a lifeless star.

And more than just your physical body, you have a soul. You can know. You can love.

As big as the mountains are, can they know someone? As big as an ocean is, can it love? As big as a galaxy is, can it will to change directions? No. But you can.

More than anything in creation you're the mirror image of God. You stand apart from everything, and you'll still be around long after all of this has passed.

Sure, you're *physically* small in this universe, but when you think about the ways you stand out from the rest of creation, you're kind of a big deal.

"PRAYER IS THE PLACE OF REFUGE FOR EVERY
WORRY, A FOUNDATION FOR CHEERFULNESS,
A SOURCE OF CONSTANT HAPPINESS,
A PROTECTION AGAINST SADNESS."

—ST. JOHN CHRYSOSTOM

Think for a moment about the two TRILLION galaxies in the universe.
Think of how small you are, physically, in the midst of all that.
Then think about what it means that spiritually you are far "bigger."

All too often people go through life feeling like they don't matter.
Do something today to remind another person that he or she is
a big deal to you, even something as simple as a text to a friend
telling her you're offering up your day in prayer for her.

I AM *Sacred*

"Do you not know that you are God's temple?"

—1 CORINTHIANS 3:16

*I*n the "cleansing of the Temple," Jesus overturned the money changers' tables and told them to stop making his Father's house a den of thieves.

You're a temple too, you know. God's word tells us, "Do you not know that your bodies are temples of the Holy Spirit?"

When I was first teaching my son about modesty he saw a billboard of an almost naked woman and said, "That's gross, right, dad?" "No, son. That's not gross." I said, "We turn our eyes from that because our bodies are too sacred and too beautiful to be thrown on a billboard as an advertisement for something."

God doesn't have "hang ups" about our sins because he thinks they're "gross." He hates our sins because they're not worthy of us. In faithfulness to Jesus' teaching, the Church teaches about purity, not out of prudishness, but because the body is too good, too beautiful, and too meaningful to be cheapened by sin.

Whether it is sins of the flesh or any other sin we are struggling with, it is critical to keep in mind that we should hate sin because it is beneath us. Our sins are cheap candy served on fine china at a royal feast. It's not good enough for us.

That perspective shift brings our battles with sin from an experience of self-loathing to an experience of striving for fulfillment. It transforms our confessions from an experience of beating ourselves up to building ourselves up.

So when you consider your failings, consider them in light of the sacredness God sees in you. You're his temple, you know. That's why he's passionate about cleansing you.

"WE ARE NOT THE SUM OF OUR WEAKNESSES AND FAILURES; WE ARE THE SUM OF THE FATHER'S LOVE FOR US."

—ST. JOHN PAUL II

Your body is sacred. Do you treat it that way? Do something to care for your body today, whether working out for fifteen minutes or taking a nice bath, and as you do that, thank God for the gift of your body.

Spend a moment thinking about the most beautiful church you've ever been in. Now...that's how God sees you.

I AM
a Child of God

*"See what love the Father has given us, that we should
be called children of God; and so we are."*

—1 JOHN 3:1

*I*nfants don't learn their identity by looking in a mirror. They learn it first by looking at mom and dad. And if you were adopted you learn that from your parents who adopted you. A parent's loving gaze says, "You are precious. You are worth dying for. Not because of what you can accomplish (because an infant can't accomplish anything!), but because you're mine."

That's called "unconditional love." It's love without limits. And communicating that is the vocation of every parent. And while we might try, none of us fulfills that vocation perfectly. My mother used to pray over me when I slept, asking God to fill the gaps in her love with his own divine love (though my Irish mother left very little gaps!). I pray the same over my children.

When the message of conditional love is written in our hearts, a voice rises from that void into adulthood. The voice says, "You're not enough. You're not pretty enough, skinny enough, rich enough, strong enough, or successful enough. You'll never be quite enough. Maybe if you perform or succeed at X, Y, and Z, *then* you'll be enough. *Then* you'll be worthy of love."

That's a lie, and it leads to a life of endless striving.

God's love isn't dependent on our perfection, it's the result of his. "He loved us first" (I John 4:19). He loves us based on our *being*, not our *doing*. He loves us even if what we're doing is terrible and wrong. "While we were sinners he died for us" (Romans 5:8). We might hide from his love, but our sins aren't powerful enough to stop his love any more than a beach umbrella is powerful enough to stop the sun from shining.

If we forget that, Christianity gets corrupted with the idea that we're using our own strength to climb our way up to God. Our virtue gets poisoned with the biggest vice of all: a pride that would think we can buy our ticket to heaven.

INSTEAD OF PRAYING WITH THE USUAL
STREAM OF WORDS, HAVE YOU EVER JUST
SAT AND ENVISIONED THE FATHER'S GAZE
UPON YOU? CLOSE YOUR EYES AND THINK OF
HIS EYES LOOKING LOVINGLY AT YOU TODAY.
YOU'RE HIS CHILD. YOU'RE ENOUGH.

A Christian should strive for perfection **because** *God loves us, not* **so** *that God will love us. Think about the ways you have strived for perfection in order to feel worthy of the praise of God, or another person. How does it make you feel when you do that?*

Take a few minutes and breathe in, "Lord Jesus…", and breathe out, "thank you for loving me as I am."

I AM *Glorified*

"*I consider that the sufferings of this present time are not worth comparing with the glory that is to be revealed in us.*"

—ROMANS 8:18

*I*t's easy for moms to feel unappreciated. In part, that's because it's hard for kids to express themselves and say just how much people mean to them.

We have a beautiful family tradition. At every birthday we take turns saying something positive about the person whose birthday we're celebrating. (Please steal this idea.) On December 18th, my wife had her turn. My son, like most teenage boys, is going through a "strong, silent type" phase. He put his hand on his forehead as if in pain, looked at his mom, and said, "I...like...I just don't know how I'm ever gonna find someone as good as you to marry...you know?"

Through my wife's tears I saw a glimmer of glory in her eyes. She had been honored—thanked for what she does, and more, for who she is. It was a small glimpse of the weight of glory awaiting her in heaven—not the glory of a decorated soldier or Olympian crossing the finish line, but the glory waiting for a mom and anyone who lives a life consisting mostly of un-praised service to others.

The most highly honored human being in the Church (not including Jesus Christ...the human being who also happens to be God) isn't a super apostle, great prophet, or warrior-king. It's a mom, who received little fanfare in this life, and is now called *Queen of Heaven and Earth*, and *Mother of God*.

The world might not see it, but there's glory waiting for you... and even now, it's in seed form, within you.

"The Lord will make you the head, and not the tail."

—DEUTERONOMY 28:13

*Get intentional about doing small things for the glory of God.
Before you sit to fold that laundry, pray, "Lord Jesus, I offer
what I am about to do in union with your offering to the Father,
by the power of the Holy Spirit, and for the salvation of the world!"
That prayer makes small acts of service a big deal.*

*Perform a random act of kindness today in secret—
knowing that God sees you. Do something extra kind
without even telling anyone else that you did it.*

DAY 24

I AM *Honorable*

*"Let no one despise your youth, but set the believers an
example in speech and conduct, in love, in faith, in purity."*

—1 TIMOTHY 4:12

The shortest homily I've ever heard was from Fr. Gus, a legendary old friar at my alma mater, Franciscan University of Steubenville. He walked slowly to the pulpit, looked out at the congregation and said, "Negative humor is from hell. Leave it there." And then he sat back down.

I'll never forget that homily!

Sarcasm comes from the Greek words *sarx* and *chasm* which together literally mean "to tear flesh." In small doses, sarcasm can be fun. However, when we're with people who go a little too far, a little too often in tearing us down with their "humor," we don't feel safe around them any more. We start to forget our dignity. If someone's negative humor begins to bother you, tell them!

And don't forget the power of your words too. It isn't hard to rip someone down. It's also not hard to build people up, so be sure you do it! If you think a friend is great at his job, that your cantor has a beautiful voice, that your pastor gave a great homily, that your spouse barbecues the best burger on the planet (though you would be wrong because I do), and that your son is amazing at football—tell them! Brag about them in front of others! Breathe life into people with your words.

It usually comes back to us when we do! People love to promote and honor those who don't hold back in honoring them. But don't just do that to get ahead. Do it because we live in a world that's too quick to tear down and too slow to build up. And the more you practice honoring others with your words, the better you'll get at doing it for yourself.

"WE SHOULD ASK OURSELVES THREE QUESTIONS BEFORE WE SPEAK: IS IT TRUE? IS IT KIND? DOES IT GLORIFY CHRIST?"

—REVEREND BILLY GRAHAM

Take a moment to review how you used words to tear down or build up others this past week. How did that make others and you feel? Be sure you approach anyone you may have hurt and apologize.

Honor someone. Look for an opportunity to praise someone this week. It can be as simple as praising your child for something in front of his siblings, or a note to someone's boss saying what a great job they did for you as a customer. If you do this kind of thing often, you'll see how it changes your perception of yourself.

I AM Beautiful

"How beautiful you are, my beloved! Oh, how beautiful!"

—SONG OF SONGS 4:1

When I was young, an older man and I were having a conversation. He was someone I admired. I made a rude comment that a certain woman was "ugly." His response caught me off guard. He was angry. "Never say that again," he said. "Every woman is beautiful. Every one." He was right, and I haven't used that word ever since.

In our own way, we are all very, very beautiful, more beautiful than mountains and oceans and spiraling galaxies. Do you perceive that in others? Do you perceive it in yourself? God does.

Much of what makes beautiful people beautiful is that they know it. They carry themselves differently. It's something more than facial structure, it's the brightness of the eyes, gentle confidence of the voice, uprightness of the back. It's the "posture" of a flower that opens up because "I have something to give" is in its DNA. We should all have that posture. When that's in your spirit, what's in your physical DNA isn't as important.

Lisa Velasquez was voted "world's ugliest woman" on a cruel YouTube video that went viral. She suffers from a rare disease that prevents her from gaining weight, blinded her in one eye, and causes premature aging. She stumbled upon the video at the age of seventeen and it wrecked her. She wanted to die. But it also forced her to dig deep and question where she got her sense of self from. Since seeing that video, she's launched a career as a motivational speaker and her videos about true beauty have impacted millions more than the cruel video that got her started! And the striking thing is, despite her disorder, her confidence sends out an undeniable message: I am beautiful!

When we walk around thinking that we're beautiful, it sends a message that convinces those around us that we are. And rightly so. Because it's true.

I tell my daughters they are beautiful so often that when young men tell them so, they're thinking, "I know, dad's been saying that my whole life!" They're not swept off their feet so easily! They are beautiful indeed! And one of the reasons they send that "beauty vibe" out to the world is that their parents have helped convince them of it. But I'm also well aware that there's a sense of dignity, royalty, and beauty that I can't give them as their dad. They have to find it in God. They have to claim it for themselves. And so do you.

**"NO ONE CAN MAKE YOU FEEL INFERIOR
WITHOUT YOUR CONSENT."**

—ELEANOR ROOSEVELT

Think of a quality that you like about yourself, even a simple physical quality. Spend a moment thanking God for it.

What would change in your life for the better if you felt like a beautiful person? Pray for the grace to see yourself that way. God does.

I AM *Pure*

"Then neither do I condemn you."

—JOHN 8:11

The book of Revelation calls the devil "the Accuser" (see Revelation 12:10). He is the first to rush over to us when we're on the ground and convince us that we're no better than the sin we just committed, or the bad experience we just had. He labels us by our sins, and he has no shortage of help from the gossips of the world. And all too often, we believe him.

False identities can follow us well into adulthood. "Sure, I might be a homeschooling mom now, but I know the *real* me. There's something filthy at my core because of what I did at that party freshman year, all those years ago." Or perhaps, more tragically, you believe the lie that, "There's something broken and impure in me because of what someone else did to me."

The woman caught in adultery in John 8 was caught in a lie that almost took her life. She was about to be executed for her sin. (Funny how the man caught in adultery wasn't about to be stoned to death. Double standards have been around for a long time.)

The woman didn't protest. She wore her name well. She thought, "I am dirty. I am trash. My entire town has seen who I am. They've given me a name. Kill me."

There, staring at the ground and waiting for the first stone to crash into her head, she saw a man's feet walk up close beside her. His shadow covered her as he addressed the crowd that had come to label and murder her.

"Let him who is without sin among you be the first to throw a stone at her" (John 8:6–8).

One by one she heard the stones thud as they hit the ground. She heard their feet shuffle away, until there was silence.

Stunned, she looked up at the stranger who had saved her life. His expression was unlike what she'd seen from other men. Men who reduced her to an object.

"Is there anyone left who condemns you?" he asked.

Her executioners had all departed. It was obviously just the two of them. So, who was he referring to when he asked if anyone there was still condemning her? I think he was referring to her. "Do *you* still condemn yourself?"

His eyes, full of respect, begged the answer. "No sir."

"Then neither do I condemn you. Go and sin no more."

The woman wasn't given her life back. She was given a new life. And Jesus had made it clear that she had a role in claiming that new life. She had to make a choice not to condemn herself, and to work on aligning her behavior with her new identity.

You're in the quiet of your room now. The people who have labeled you aren't there now. The ones who have hurt you have moved on with their lives. The high school gossips have all dropped their stones and walked away. It's just you and Jesus.

Is there anyone there who condemns you?

Ask Jesus to help you name the condemnation you carry because of past sin—either committed by you or to you.

Remember, failure is an event, not a person. Your sins are a page, not the story. Decide right now to choose not to condemn yourself and say out loud "I am free and pure because of Jesus' love for me." And every time you feel broken and dirty inside, say it out loud again.

I AM *Important*

"He has anointed me to proclaim good news to the poor."

—LUKE 4:18

I recently filmed an episode for our TV show *Real Life Catholic* to highlight Denver's homeless and the ways the Church is serving them. All my preconceived notions about homelessness were smashed that day. I had thought most homeless people were addicts or struggled with mental illness. The reality is that most of them came upon hard times, no family or friends rose up to help, and after being stuck in their situation long enough, they stopped fighting it and tried to make peace with a new lifestyle on the streets. Most of them feel forgotten and invisible.

The missionaries I worked with from Christ in the City told me their mission wasn't just to feed and clothe the homeless, it was to give them back their sense of dignity and to remind them that they're humans—that they matter. They walk the streets every day meeting the homeless, making eye contact, learning their names, and becoming their friends.

St. Teresa of Calcutta said the poverty of wealthy nations is more painful than what she saw in Calcutta, where people are literally starving to death on the sidewalks. "The spiritual poverty of the Western world is much greater than the physical poverty of our people. You, in the West, have millions of people who suffer such terrible loneliness and emptiness. They feel unloved and unwanted."

As I served the homeless, I realized how thin the line is that divides "us" from "them." We all long to be loved, noticed, cherished, and told that we matter. When we become convinced that we aren't, something within us starts to die and fade away.

The great paradox is that when we get out of our heads and decide to remind other people how precious they are, we realize how important we are in the process. We are the hands and feet of God. We are his voice proclaiming good news to the poor. We are the fiery presence of God warming a cold world. We are important.

"Give, and it will be given to you; good measure, pressed down, shaken together, running over, will be put into your lap. For the measure you give will be the measure you get back."

—LUKE 6:38

Reflecting on your life, list the opportunities God has given you to interact with the poor and/or how you remind other people how precious they are to you. How did that make you feel?

Do something for someone who can't pay you back. Contact your local parish to learn more about local opportunities to serve the poor, and today, put something on your calendar this month!

I AM *Blessed*

"For I know the plans I have for you, says the Lord, plans for welfare and not for evil, to give you a future and a hope."

—JEREMIAH 29:11

I've had many moments in life where I ask, "Why me?" not in the negative sense, but rather, "Why all the blessings!? I'm not worthy!" I usually feel that gratitude in the simple moments, like after a great day with my family, while eating a really good meal, or soaking in natural beauty.

But those moments are often tainted by a creeping suspicion. When things are going really well, I'm often waiting for the bomb to drop. The poet William Butler Yeats wrote that the Irish have an abiding sense of tragedy that sustains them through temporary periods of joy. I'm half Irish! I love that about myself. But I hate that inner voice that whispers, "Don't get used to the good times. There's gotta be some 'trade off.' Everybody's gotta pay the piper."

Of course, there's some truth in that. We all die in the end, so everyone has to leave it all. But the trick Jesus played on death is that "the end" isn't really the end. It's the beginning of eternal blessedness. He paid the piper for us.

Christians shouldn't live life waiting for the bomb that's about to drop. You should live ready for the blessing about to drop. The blessed moments you have are a glimpse of what's waiting for you. Forever. Blessings don't come to pass. Problems come to pass. Your blessings come to stay. When you're feeling blessed, that's God saying, "I have an eternity of unmerited blessing upon blessing waiting for you. I created you for this. Get used to it."

"You bless the righteous, O Lord. You cover him with favor as with a shield."

—PSALM 5:12

Spend time thinking about heaven. If you could invent your perfect heaven, what would it look like?

Consider that St. Paul wrote about heaven that what God has prepared for those who love him is so great it hasn't even entered man's mind. That means whatever you imagine heaven to be won't compare with what God has prepared for you! Rest in the knowledge that with every passing minute, you get closer to your true home, one that moth and rust cannot destroy (see Matthew 6:20).

I AM Worthy

"Come with me by yourselves to a quiet place and rest a while."

—MARK 6:31

esus said "love your neighbor as yourself" (Mark 12:31). He was presuming that his followers love themselves! And love is expressed in actions, not just feelings. Do you love yourself in your actions? Do you treat yourself with love?

I came home from a trip recently and my wife was absolutely burnt out. I didn't say "Drop, give me ten Rosaries and get those dishes done." (Of course, if I had said that, those dishes may have come flying at me!) I was moved with compassion and, in one of my finer moments as a husband, I said, "Stay right there. Let me run out and get you some sushi." And it struck me: if our Lord walked into the room at that moment, he would probably have said the same thing!

We think that God is only concerned about "spiritual" things, but that our basic needs like rest, cleanliness, food, or even the little things that inspire us and make us happy are somehow beneath him. That idea isn't from Scripture. It's not from God. We have a God who loves to take care of our basic human needs!

We have a God who washed his apostles' feet. In one encounter they had with him after he rose, they found Jesus on the beach cooking them breakfast. There are many layers of theological meaning to that fish breakfast, but one layer of meaning was this: He wanted to cook them a nice breakfast. After he made someone rise from the dead and caused a huge commotion, he would generally cut through the chaos with a profound phrase like this: "Get him something to eat." In other words: "The poor kid was dead. He needs a sandwich."

God takes our small and very human needs very seriously. On one level that's because it's so hard to grow spiritually if those needs aren't met. Don't complicate things: If you can't pray well, have you been sleeping enough? If you're feeling too drained to care for someone else, have you worked out or taken a walk or read a book or done anything that would qualify as "self care" lately? If you're a new mom and feeling totally burnt out, have you gotten a shower in lately!?

I know, the demands of life make you feel selfish when you take a break from studying, working, or taking care of the kids to get "me time." But ironically, when you don't care for yourself, all you leave your loved ones with is the most burnt out version of yourself. There's nothing loving about that. And if you're a parent, you're teaching your children that you lack the dignity and self-worth to spend time on yourself, and that teaches them about their own dignity and worth.

So if not for your own sake, love yourself for the sake of those who love you! You don't have to be rich to read a good book, enjoy a meal, watch a movie, work out, take time to soak in an extra long shower, or take a nap. You just have to claim the truth that you're worth it, and then claim the time to do it.

———— ⌘ ————

"Whatever is true, whatever is honorable, whatever is just, whatever is pure, whatever is lovely, whatever is gracious, if there is any excellence, if there is anything worthy of praise, think about these things."

—PHILIPPIANS 4:8

———— ⌘ ————

Do you feel selfish when you spend time on yourself?
Who in your life is the source of that lie? They might have been
well intentioned, but they were wrong. Stop listening to them.

Write down one thing that feeds your spirit or inspires
you that you've been neglecting to do lately. Then put
it in your calendar and make sure you do it!

I AM *Attractive*

"The spirit of man is the lamp of the Lord."

—PROVERBS 20:27

I fly somewhere in the world every week, and every once in a while I see a toddler board the plane who you would swear owned the airline. They're sure to make eye contact with every passenger on the long journey to their seats with a smile almost says, "Hi! And welcome to my plane!" They walk through life with hearts wide open. Most of us start out that way.

Things happen along the rocky journey of life that convinces us to close our hearts. A spouse cheats on you, someone you have a crush on doesn't return your interest, a friend turns on you, you lose a job, a bully targets you, and the lie creeps in: "I'm not attractive. I have nothing of worth to give. I need to turn in on myself to be safe."

Jesus teaches us that someone's rejection of us, or even cruelty toward us, should have zero impact on our joyful and generous posture toward the world. "You, therefore, must be perfect, as your heavenly Father is perfect. For he makes his sun rise on the evil and on the good, and sends rain on the just and on the unjust" (Matthew 5:48, 45).

Don't let anything deprive the world of who you are. And don't let anyone deprive you of the joy of being a generous, loving, kind, joyful person. Don't let anyone deprive you of the joy of being a blessing!

A flower doesn't close its petals if a bee passes by it. That's the bee's loss. That flower knows it has something to give. God gave you qualities that only you can give. He gave a heart that only you can love with. Be confident. Stay open.

The spiritual life starts with a heart open wide to reality. Joy starts there too. Don't let anyone take that from you.

"IF YOU HEAR A VOICE WITHIN YOU SAY
'YOU CANNOT PAINT,' THEN BY ALL MEANS
PAINT, AND THAT VOICE WILL BE SILENCED."

—VINCENT VAN GOGH

*Is there a particular person or situation that you regularly allow
to steal your joy? Offer a prayer that God blesses him or her!*

*Be ready: Decide before you get around that person or scenario
that you aren't going to let it rob you of your peace, joy, and love.
Envision how you are going to act rightly, and then follow through.*

I AM *Not Alone*

"Even though I walk through the valley of the shadow of death, I will fear no evil, for you are with me."

—PSALM 23:4

*E*veryone feels lonely at times, but the truth is "alone" is a lie. It has never existed. Even in the abyss before space and time, there was the Trinity: One God who is a communion of three Persons. And not only is he with you, he's surrounded you with angels and saints.

When Elisha the prophet was surrounded by an army that wanted to kill him, he was calm and cool. His servant was terrified until he was given a vision. He saw horses and chariots of fire all around Elisha! He realized they were far from alone. They were surrounded by an unseen army. So are you.

You might be in a hospital bed, away from home for the first time, a new parent caring for someone all day who can't carry on an adult conversation with you, experiencing a broken relationship, grieving the death of a spouse, or feeling rejected because of your faith. The truth is that you're part of the Church, the Body of Christ on earth today.

You're spiritually connected with people all over the world struggling just as you are. You're surrounded by angels. A multitude that's already crossed the finish line is cheering you on. You're far from alone.

And you have Jesus at your side. He experienced the pain of isolation many times throughout his life, but especially on the Cross. Shortly before he breathed his last he looked up to heaven and shouted out, "My God, why have you forsaken me?" That means that when you're in your darkest moments and want to cry out, "God, where are you?" you're not saying those words alone. Even then, he is with you, saying those words right beside you, so you would have someone to say it with.

"Can a mother forget her infant, be without tenderness for the child of her womb? Even should she forget, I will never forget you. See, upon the palms of my hands I have engraved you..."

—ISAIAH 49:15-16

What circumstances make you feel alone and forgotten?

The next time you feel alone, spend a moment thinking of the angels and saints who surround you and cheer you on, no less than they surrounded Elisha!

I AM *Delightful*

*"He will rejoice over you with gladness, he will renew you
in his love; he will exult over you with loud singing."*

—ZEPHANIAH 3:17

"*G*od loves you." We've all heard that so many times it has become background noise. I mean, of course he loves me. It's his job. He is God. He *has* to love me. But does he *like* me? Probably not. He would like me if I were the *me* I know I'm supposed to be. He would like me if...

WRONG.

God doesn't only love you, he likes you. And more: He delights in you!

You've heard the phrase, "You're one in a million." Actually, that's a massive understatement. When you consider that a woman reaches adulthood with about 400,000 eggs, and a male produces 200 million sperm cells per day, the odds of *you* on a given day are about 1 in 80 trillion. Then when you consider that if your great cavemen grandparents 10,000 years ago hadn't met, or perhaps had met a month later than they did, you wouldn't be here, the odds of you existing are far smaller than 1 in 80 trillion. And yet God summed *you* from the void into the light of existence.

Congratulations!

And why did he summon you into being from nothingness? Because the idea of you delighted him before time began.

Before your mother even knew you were there, his eyes were on you. As the Psalmist says, "For you created my inmost being; you knit me together in my mother's womb" (Psalm 139:13–14).

There is a way that only you can see and experience life, serve humanity, tell a joke, or hear a song, and that delights God. There is a way that only you can glorify God forever, and that delights him too. Every diamond receives and reflects light in a way that's completely unique. That's also true of us. In some sense, we'll add to the glory of God forever by receiving and reflecting his divine life in a way that is uniquely Ben, Kandyce, Andy, Gabby, Sylvia, YOU.

I know you have an image of the you that you *should* be— and who God is calling you to become. That's good. Dream. Strive. Change. Grow. But once that vision ruins your peace today, you can know that the devil's lies and an unhealthy pride just got mixed in with God's dreams for you.

I have dreams for my toddler as she grows up, but do you think I'm not enjoying her today? I delight in her! *The ways she needs to grow* don't sum up my vision of who she is! As you strive to grow, don't forget to love, and even to *like* the person that you are today. God does.

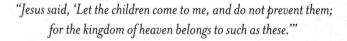

"Jesus said, 'Let the children come to me, and do not prevent them; for the kingdom of heaven belongs to such as these.'"

—MATTHEW 19:14

*Removing all pride, striving, and defenses, honestly
ask yourself, "Do I like myself?" If not, why?*

*Think about the "moment" before space and time when God first thought
of you and decided you would be. Why do you think he chose you?*

I AM *the Light*

*"You are the light of the world. A city
set on a mountain cannot be hidden."*

—MATTHEW 5:14

"**You** are the light of the world." That sounds like a line from Scripture about God, but it's not. It's about you. Jesus said that to his followers.

You are the light of the world!

"Me?!" You ask. "I understand Jesus saying that about my priest, or a famous person, or a missionary, or a saint, or perhaps a teacher. Not me. I'm not important."

Have you ever considered that most of Jesus' life wasn't "important" or noticed by worldly standards? He spent thirty years as a small-town carpenter. After launching his mission, he didn't venture more than a few hundred miles from the place where he was born, and during his three-year public ministry his message didn't reach millions. It reached thousands.

The Gospels stand apart from most great historic or religious books because they're so strikingly insignificant from a worldly point of view. Matthew, Mark, Luke, and John aren't about conquering armies or people in places of power. They're full of stories about Jesus encountering average people and working amazing, but relatively small miracles from a worldly point of view. Who cares if a blind beggar in Palestine in AD 32 can now see, or a girl who would go on to eventually die again was raised from the dead, or a wedding party had enough wine? The Gospels answer that question—God does.

Maybe God was showing us that there are no small acts of service because there's no such thing as an average person or insignificant life. Every human being is of infinite worth to our infinite God! That means the way you bring in the light of God to the people you encounter every day is of unfathomable importance, and so are you.

God loves us so much that he doesn't only invite us to follow him, but anoints us to do as he does, and more: to be who he is for the people we encounter every day, in big and small ways. Christian means "Christ-like."

God has made you the light because the world is in darkness. He has filled you with himself because the world is hungry. He has revealed his fatherly love to you because the world has forgotten its true identity. He has anointed you because the world needs Christ.

You have no idea how important you are. You are the light of the world.

"Be renewed in the spirit of your minds, and put on the new nature, created after the likeness of God in true righteousness and holiness."

—EPHESIANS 4:23-24

Reflect on what aspects of your personality and gifts you think the words "light of the world" apply the most to.

What sins, distractions, vices, or self-doubts stop those things from shining as brightly as they could?

NOW... *Your Homework!*

1. RE-READ THIS BOOK UNTIL YOU BELIEVE IT

I suppose I could have written hundreds of "I AM" meditations, but I always opt to keep things simple. I believe in a God who keeps things simple. God didn't write long books to the world. The Bible is a series of booklets that we're supposed to read and re-read until we "get it." Re-read your new, God-given names in this book again and again until you believe them.

2. RENOUNCE YOUR FALSE NAMES

Jesus called the Holy Spirit "the Advocate." An advocate is one who builds you up. He's got your back. And he'll go to bat for you. The opposite of an advocate is an accuser. An accuser rips you down. The book of Revelation calls the devil "the Accuser."

You are in the midst of an epic spiritual battle between the Advocate and the Accuser. The front line is your thinking. Whose side are you on?

Decide to side with the Advocate. Don't underestimate the power of your will. God won't force his joy, freedom, peace, and love on you. You have to chose it.

"We take captive every thought to make it obedient to Christ" (2 Corinthians 10:5). Name the lies you've been believing, overtly renounce them, and fill in the gap with God's truth about who you are.

Spend some time writing down the negative names you've given yourself over the years in the chart provided on the next page under the column entitled "Lie"—perhaps things that jumped out at you as you read the meditations in this book. Then use your pen to cross out the lie.

Then, think of the opposite of that lie. Write it down in the column next to your lie under the heading "Truth." Then take this sheet to prayer, and out loud, say "Lord Jesus, in your name and by your power and authority I renounce the lie that I am [insert your lies here, one at a time]. I claim the truth that I am [insert your new names here]."

Make a decision to continue rejecting that lie and replacing it with the truth whenever it arises in your mind, whenever feelings associated with that lie take hold in your gut, or whenever old patterns of behavior that are rooted in that lie appear in your life.

This is a war. You need to be vigilant. The Enemy won't ever stop trying to bring you down. Do not give him any permission or any foothold. The Accuser is powerless when you decide to side with the Advocate! In fact, he's already lost the war and he knows it. In Romans 8:37, St. Paul tells us that "we are more than conquerors" in Christ Jesus. Start living in your victory, my friend!

I AM

LIE	TRUTH
dirty	pure
out of control	powerful and peaceful

3. IDENTIFY YOUR PRIMARY LIE AND CLAIM YOUR PRIMARY NAME

You've reflected on new and life-giving names and identified false and life-draining labels. Now let's dig a little deeper.

I believe there is a *primary lie* that the Evil One wants you to believe that directly opposes your greatest gift, calling, and charism.

People who have seen me speak in public would probably never guess that I've battled with a lot of insecurity. I used to struggle with constantly second-guessing myself and with a nagging feeling that I don't "measure up." My every stage appearance was preceded by a visit to the bathroom for many years! And my mission was often misguided by attempts to be what other people in ministry were, while God was calling me to do something entirely unique for his kingdom. I'm happy to say that's in the past.

The Accuser knew I would be teaching priests, advising bishops, and reaching millions. God was calling me to lead and that's exactly where the devil attacked me. I countered his lie that *I am inadequate* with the truth that *I am a king!*

What is your primary lie? Revisit the list you wrote out in the previous page and underline that lie. The other lies are probably rooted in it. What name do you need to speak into that lie the most? *Write it on the chart in all capital letters!* It's crucial to identify the name you need to remember most and repeat it to yourself often!

4. SERVE

When a star collapses, it gets incredibly dense, making its gravitational pull even stronger. This causes it to cave in on itself more deeply, which makes it denser, which makes its gravitational pull stronger...and so the process goes on and on. Upon their deaths, smaller stars assume their place in the universe as white dwarfs—a cool flicker in space. Massive stars collapse until they become black holes—a place where the gravitational pull is so strong that literally everything that comes within *the point of no return*—known as the "event horizon"—is pulled in, even light.

A soul is mightier than a ball of gas in the sky. Every person either emanates light to a dark world, or pulls it in to themselves. Most of us have our "black hole days" where if anyone gets within our personal "event horizon" we pull a little light from them.

Philippians 2:15 tells us that God's children are to "shine like stars in the night sky." When we derive our identity and our sense of worth from him, we're no longer pulling from everyone else to fill up something that's lacking in us. We're able to give. We're able to shine.

You have meditated on the names God gives you to build you up. But his purpose for building you up isn't to inflate you, it's to send you. People who know themselves are able to give themselves. And people who give themselves come to know themselves more deeply and to shine more brightly. Such is the reverse spiritual law of the black hole!

How is God calling you to make a gift of yourself? Where the world's needs and your gifts intersect is where you're called. Reflect on your unique strengths, gifts, and passions, and decide where to bless the world with all that you are!

It doesn't have to be in "big" ways. The more important you realize you are to God the more you realize how much each human being matters too. Every person is of infinite significance to our infinite God, and that means no act of service to another human being is insignificant. Are you a good listener? How about sitting with the elderly who have no one to visit them in a home, or perhaps your lonely neighbor. Are you passionate about sharing your faith? Volunteer to teach confirmation kids at your home parish. Are you a nurturing person? Find a charity where you can serve a meal to the poor. Are you financially blessed? Give it away. Are you good with technology or organization? There are endless ways you can help a non-profit behind the scenes. There's something for everyone.

I'm not asking you to change careers, unless, of course, God is calling you to that! But keep it simple. Be intentional about serving regularly, in concrete ways. That will help you maintain the heart of a servant in your everyday life.

CALLED TO SERVE

I AM *My gifts and strengths*	I WILL *How my gift blesses others*

5. WORSHIP THE GREAT "I AM"

I brought my family on a speaking and filming trip to Hawaii. It was an amazing blessing to be able to do that. We arrived late at night, and I carried my sleeping children from the car to their bed in the beach house. I'll never forget waking up with them as the sun rose.

Without speaking, we opened our eyes and stumbled onto the beach. It was early enough that we had it completely to ourselves. Gentle waves lapped the sand as they had since that volcanic island broke sea level millions of years before. The sun bathed the horizon, and us, in hues of red, orange, and pink as it filled the sky above with light blue.

Within minutes my toddler, Clementine, had stripped herself naked and started walking with an amazed daze into the water! I could almost see the moment when, on the other side of life, she'll enter eternity. Picture being an old broken body falling asleep only to wake up flooded with new youth, and stumble out, dazed, onto the most beautiful scene imaginable.

Ecstasy comes from Greek words that literally mean "to stand outside." To be in a state of ecstasy is to be drawn outside of yourself—to lose yourself in something.

Paradoxically, it is in those times when we're drawn so utterly outside of ourselves by truth, beauty, goodness...and above all, by love, that we come to experience our true selves.

This book probably encouraged a lot of holy introspection. That's important! But don't stay there. There's a love that blazes mightier than the sun and churns deeper than the ocean and it's all aimed at you, God's little one. Set your eyes on that divine love. When we allow him to fill the horizon of our minds, everything else tends to become clear in that light, including our own identity. When we lose ourselves in him we realize who we are. "For…whoever loses his life for my sake will find it" (Matthew 16:25).

As the great St. John Paul II said, "When you wonder about the mystery of yourself, look to Christ, who gives you the meaning of life. When you wonder what it means to be a mature person, look to Christ, who is the fullness of humanity. And when you wonder about your role in the future of the world look to Christ" (Address to High School Students, Madison Square Garden, New York, Wednesday, October 3, 1979).

On that note, I thought the best way to wrap up our thirty-three meditations on names God has given you, is with thirty-three names he's given himself in Scripture—all of which reveal different aspects of the great I AM.

Spend some time worshiping God with these names. Nothing draws us from the smallness of self into the vastness of God like worship. Worship is simple. Quietly breathe in the names below and breath out "I praise you." Do it regularly.

As you fix your eyes on who God is, you'll come to see more clearly who you are, because all that is beautiful, good, and true in him is imprinted on the image of all his children.

I AM
—EXODUS 3:14, JOHN 8:58

Our Father
—MATTHEW 6:9

The Beginning
—REVELATIONS 22:13

The End
—REVELATIONS 22:13

Anointed One
—ACTS 4:26

The Way
—JOHN 14:6

The Truth
—JOHN 14:6

The Life
—JOHN 14:6

Author of Life
—ACTS 3:15

God of Peace
—1 CORINTHIANS 14:33

Gift
—JOHN 4:10

Advocate
—JOHN 14:26

Bright Morning Star
—REVELATION 22:16

Root and Offspring of David
—REVELATION 22:16

Word Made Flesh
—JOHN 1:14

The True Light
—JOHN 1:49

Wonderful Counselor
—ISAIAH 9:6

Mighty God
—ISAIAH 9:6

Everlasting Father
—ISAIAH 9:6

Prince of Peace
—ISAIAH 9:6

The Ancient of Days
—DANIEL 7:9

The Child
—MATTHEW 2:13

Good Shepherd
—JOHN 10:11

King of kings
—REVELATION 19:16, JOHN 19:21

Lord of lords
—REVELATION 19:16

The Lord Who Heals Me
—EXODUS 15:26

Bread of Life
—JOHN 6:26

My Shield
—GENESIS 15:1

Eternal
—1 TIMOTHY 1:17

Immortal
—1 TIMOTHY 1:17

He who began a good work in me
—PHILIPPIANS 1:6

Love
—1 JOHN 4:8

JESUS,
because he will save his people
—MATTHEW 1:21

ISN'T IT TIME TO START LIVING THE LIFE YOU WERE MADE FOR?

God didn't create you just to get by, he created you to live life to the full! Rediscover God and rediscover the life you were made for.

REBOOT
a life-changing event

To attend a REBOOT LIVE event with Chris Stefanick, or if you're interested in hosting one at your parish, please visit RealLifeCatholic.com

ABOUT THE AUTHOR

Chris Stefanick is an internationally acclaimed speaker, author, and TV show host, who has devoted his life to helping people discover the hope that comes from the Gospel of Jesus Christ.

Chris' live events reach more than 85,000 people per year. His TV show, videos and radio spots reach more than a million people every month.

A graduate of the Franciscan University of Steubenville, Chris is the founder and president of Real Life Catholic, a non-profit which operates as the headquarters for Chris' various initiatives. Above all, Chris is proud to be the husband to his wife, Natalie, and father to their six children.

Want to join Chris in making a difference in countless people's lives? Visit RealLifeCatholic.com to become an ambassador of hope today.

OUR MISSION

To ignite a bold, contagious faith in the heart of every Catholic in North America.

OUR WORK

We serve Christ and his Church by building a movement of Catholics who share the beauty, power, and truth of the Gospel with a world that has largely forgotten. We remind people of the best news in history through a convergence of life-changing LIVE EVENTS; MEDIA, including television, radio, online videos, books and CDs; and, various EDUCATIONAL INITIATIVES, all designed to continually nudge people toward a deeper relationship with Jesus Christ, and a greater confidence for sharing him with the world.

RealLifeCatholic.com • info@RealLifeCatholic.com